Birth of a Foal

by Jane Miller

SCHOLASTIC BOOK SERVICES
NEW YORK · TORONTO · LONDON · AUCKLAND · SYDNEY · TOKYO

The author and publisher are grateful for the
help of Mrs C. P. Blake of Court Farm, West Meon,
Hampshire, where the mare and her foal are part of the
Lippen Stud of Welsh ponies owned by Mrs Blake.

ISBN 0-590-05361-2

12 11 10 9 8 7 6

3 4 5 6 7/8

Printed in the U. S. A.

02

This is the story of the birth of Fizz, a Welsh Mountain pony, and her first few days of life.

Here she is when she is one day old.

Fizz's father is a splendid stallion.

Fizz's mother is a gray mare. She lives in a
paddock with several other ponies.

Soon the mare will give birth to her first foal. She has been carrying it in a sac in her belly for eleven months.

For a short while before the birth she feels restless. She canters around the field and scratches against the fence.

When she knows the time has come for the foal to be born, the mare finds a quiet place to be by herself.

She lies down ready to give birth. Slowly the foal appears. As the foal starts to come out, its front legs break the thin sac.

The birth takes only a few minutes. The foal lies on the ground behind her mother, wet and partly covered by the sac.

The mare looks around and sees her baby for the first time.

The mother and baby are still not quite separated. The foal is joined to the mare by an umbilical cord. While she was in her mother's belly, the foal was fed through this cord.

Fizz tries to get up, but she is still too weak. At first she falls down. Each time she tries to stand, her muscles become stronger.

Finally her struggles break the cord, and
Fizz is free.

Fizz's owner has carried her onto the grass. It is clean and comfortable there. The mare follows close behind.

A few minutes later Fizz gets to her feet and manages to stand on her wobbly legs.

Like any mother
wanting to show off
her newborn baby,
the mare introduces
Fizz to the pony in
the next field.

Fizz begins to feel
hungry. Her mother
helps her find the
udder full of milk,
and the foal quickly
learns to suck.

The mare is also hungry and starts to graze. Fizz sets off for a walk by herself. She is still unsteady on her legs.

It has been a busy afternoon. The mare is
tired and lies down to rest. She makes sure
that Fizz is licked clean and dry. Before
long they are both asleep.

Fizz is now three days old. Her mother takes her for a walk. They climb a small hill.

Then they canter around the field with the other ponies.

Fizz spends much of the time sleeping on the grass in the warm spring sunshine. Then she scrambles to her feet and dozes standing up. Her mother is never very far away.

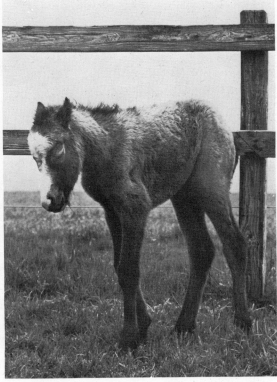

When Fizz wakes up, she yawns and stretches
her jaws.

She uses her legs to
scratch.

Sometimes the itchy
place is difficult to
reach.

When Fizz feels hungry, she butts her mother's belly and then sucks milk from her udder.

Stretching helps her discover her muscles. Fizz is growing stronger.

When her mother lies down to rest,
Fizz usually wants to play.

The mare and foal spend many hours
nuzzling. They are getting to know
each other.

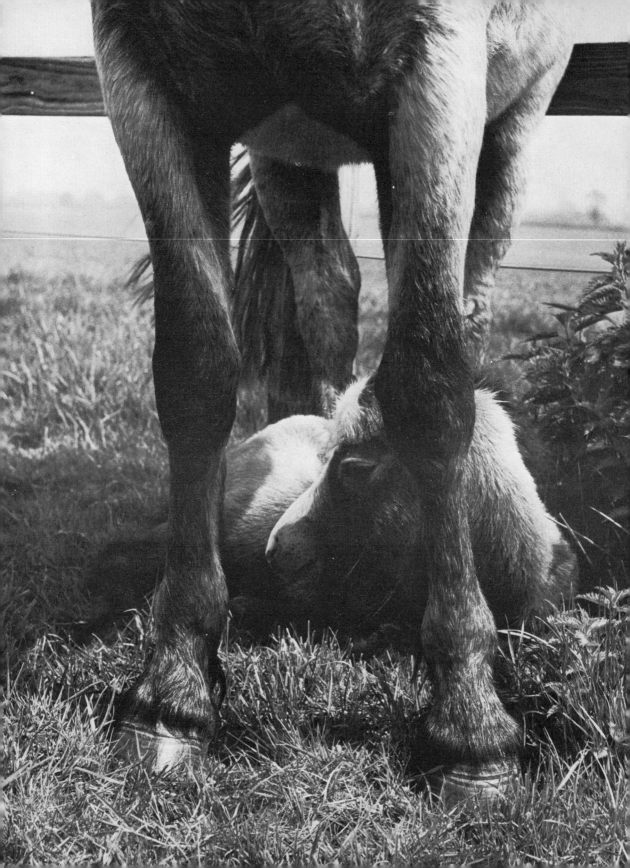

When the sun is hot, Fizz rests
in her mother's shade.

She watches her mother graze.

The mare is very fond of her foal.

The wind is cold
in early spring.
Fizz finds that
the warmest place
is under her
mother's belly.

But she still spends most of her time eating and sleeping.

Sometimes drops of milk spill all over her face.

The mare's tail switches away the flies. Fizz's fluffy tail is still too short to be useful.

Sometimes Fizz leaves her mother to explore the field on her own.

She is becoming stronger and more
independent. She learns about life
on the farm.

For the first six months of her life Fizz will
need her mother's milk. After that she will be
weaned and able to feed herself.